Historic England

GW00493964

Hampshire

Philip MacDougall

AMBERLEY

First published 2019

Amberley Publishing
The Hill, Stroud, Gloucestershire, GL5 4EP
www.amberley-books.com

Copyright © Philip MacDougall, 2019

The right of Philip MacDougall to be identified
as the Author of this work has been asserted in
accordance with the Copyright, Designs and Patents
Act 1988.

The publisher is grateful to the staff at Historic England
who gave the time to review this book.

All contents remain the responsibility of the publisher.

ISBN 978 1 4456 9129 9 (print)
ISBN 978 1 4456 9130 5 (ebook)

All rights reserved. No part of this book may be
reprinted or reproduced or utilised in any form or by
any electronic, mechanical or other means, now known
or hereafter invented, including photocopying and
recording, or in any information storage or retrieval
system, without the permission in writing from the
Publishers.

British Library Cataloguing in Publication Data.
A catalogue record for this book is available from the
British Library.

Typesetting by Aura Technology and Software
Services, India. Printed in Great Britain.

Contents

Introduction

This book covers the area of Hampshire before Southampton and Portsmouth were made unitary authorities, but does not include Bournemouth nor the Isle of Wight, which were both at one time encompassed within the administrative area of the county. Both Portsmouth and Southampton have already been the subject of separate books in this same series, but these two cities are included when their story is part of the wider Hampshire story. In putting the book together, I have followed several particular themes, rather than attempting to make this a general history of the county. These themes reflect the nature of the ceremonial county of Hampshire and certain significant events in its history.

Away from the big cities, Hampshire is a county with a considerable rural expanse, giving rise to a theme that looks at villages and grand houses to be found in the countryside. The importance of the county's religious institutions is also explored. Winchester had the richest bishopric in the entire country during medieval times and in the Bishop of Winchester one of the wealthiest and most powerful of clerics, with his influence stretching far and wide.

Through its lengthy coastline, a further facet of the county had to be explored: the need to provide a robust defence against seaborne invasion in the form of numerous castles and fortresses. Here, the starting point is archaeology and the prehistoric hill forts and Roman defences depicted in that segment, with a later section that moves forward in time, looking at the coastal defence castles built by Henry VIII, as well as the later Georgian and Victorian fortifications built to overpower any planned attack on Portsmouth.

A section of contrasts is the final one, devoted to work and leisure. Here, the dissimilarity of work performed in the many small rural villages of the county, where farming and industries related to it were the only employers, is contrasted with the huge industrial conurbations that were, and still are, to be found elsewhere in the county.

Archaeology

St Catherine's Hill Hill Fort, Winchester
Hampshire has a large number of Iron Age hill forts. This aerial view of the hill fort on
St Catherine's Hill was taken in 1949. It is approximately 23 acres. Part excavations in the late
1920s indicated that the hilltop had originally formed an unfortified Iron Age settlement, dated
550–450 BCE, before the defences were constructed in the the third century BCE and finally
abandoned in the first century BCE. (© Historic England Archive. Aerofilms Collection)

Opposite: Calleva Atrebatum, Silchester
The remains of the Romano-British town of Calleva Atrebatum are seen here in outline in this
1949 aerial photograph, juxtaposed with an artist's impression of how the town would have
appeared during the late third century CE. Frequently the subject of archaeological investigation,
much of the Roman town has been mapped, a task made easier by the site being abandoned
shortly after the Roman departure from Britain and very limited later habitation. In the
reconstructed drawing of the town, the forum is seen towards the centre and the amphitheatre,
often used for sporting events, immediately outside the town wall. (© Historic England Archive.
Aerofilms Collection; © Historic England Archive)

Twyford Down, Earthworks

Following archaeological investigations, the earthworks to be seen on Twyford Down, on the south side of the motorway, have been interpreted as evidence of the existence of a late Romano-British farmstead or villa. Roman pottery and roofing tiles dating to the third or fourth century CE, together with a piece of tessellated pavement, are evidence of it being a community of fairly high status. (© Historic England Archive)

Roman Fortress of Portchester

Seen here in 1955 is a general view along the east side of the fortress wall of Portchester that was constructed by the Romans, with archaeological evidence indicating it was built during the third century CE and subsequently abandoned during the late fourth century. Its purpose was to guard Portsmouth harbour against raids by Saxons, Jutes and Angles from the Continent. It has the most complete walls of any Roman fort in Europe. (Historic England Archive)

Above and below: Entry into the Town of Calleva Atrebatum

An impression of how the north gate of the city of Calleva Atrebatum might have appeared, with a photograph showing the present-day remains of the south gate. Prior to the construction of a stone defensive wall during the third century CE, the town had been defended by earthen ramparts, but increasing dangers and uncertainties had prompted construction of a much stronger line of defence. Shortly after the wall was completed there is suggestion that the town was sacked by Allectus, a naval commander who attempted to rule Britain in place of the emperor in Rome. (© Historic England Archive; © Crown copyright. Historic England Archive)

Portchester Fortress, Tenth Century
Although abandoned in the late fourth century, archaeologists have shown that the area of the fortress was reused by the Saxons, with excavations revealing changes and alterations to the site at that time. This illustration, based on those archaeological findings, shows the castle as it probably appeared during the tenth century. (© Historic England Archive)

Roman Shoe
Detail of a Roman shoe found during an archaeological investigation of the Roman fortress of Portchester. (© Historic England Archive)

The Saxon Minster Winchester

Above: The Anglo-Saxon Cathedral of Winchester

Demolished in 1093, this illustration demonstrates the likely appearance of the Anglo-Saxon cathedral for the diocese of Winchester, which was built in 660 and continued in use until its demolition in 1093. Standing partly to the north and beneath the present cathedral, the site is marked in brickwork and was subject to archaeological investigation during the 1960s, with finds from the site to be seen in the Winchester City Museum. (© Historic England Archive)

Below: Site of Henry V's Warship *Grace Dieu*

Offering a unique insight into the navy of Henry V are the remains of *Grace Dieu*, a warship built in Southampton and probably launched during the summer of 1418. Lying in the mud of the River Hamble where she was struck by lightning in 1439 and burnt to the waterline, the remains have been subject to several archaeological investigations, which have confirmed *Grace Dieu* to have had a likely length of 200 feet from stem to stern. This area includes the remains of at least one other vessel of Henry V's navy, with the possible remains of the *Holigost* being particularly interesting. (© Historic England Archive)

Above: Basing House, Norman Motte and Moat
An archaeological site of several periods, the former Basing House was destroyed during the Civil War. This photograph was taken in 1885, at the time when an extensive archaeological survey was underway and shows the Norman moat and motte (rising to the left) that pre-existed the house. Further archaeological digs were carried out in the 1960s and again in 2015, with Stone Age tools and Civil War relics among the items uncovered. (Historic England Archive)

Opposite: Netley: Early Archaeological Exploration of the Medieval Abbey
The Cistercian abbey at Netley, one of the best surviving Cistercian abbeys in the country, has frequently gained the attention of archaeologists. This photograph from the 1860s shows the progress of an excavation examining the foundations of the abbey refectory that was carried out by two amateur archaeologists, Revds Edmund Kell and J. A. Addison. At that time, a building – believed to be the infirmary – was uncovered lying beneath the present-day car park. (Historic England Archive)

Royal Naval Hospital Cemetery, Haslar, Gosport
More than 20,000 seamen and marines were buried in the cemetery of the hospital during the eighteenth and early nineteenth centuries. This has provided archaeologists with an opportunity to study, using isotopic analysis of bone collagen, the nature of the eighteenth-century naval diet and whether it correlates with the historical information on the diet of naval seamen. In a study that broke new ground, a total of thirty rib specimens were analysed and showed that the naval diet, as provided by the Admiralty, was of a relatively high quality when compared with the average diet of the population at that time. (© Historic England Archive)

Abbeys and Ecclesiastical Palaces

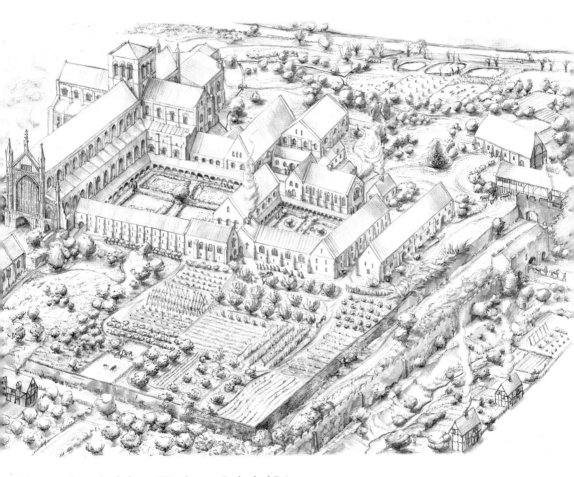

Above and overleaf above: Winchester Cathedral Priory

During the Middle Ages, Hampshire saw the establishment of a number of monastic houses. The Benedictine Winchester Cathedral Priory was both one of the earliest and most affluent – the annual income from its estates during the late fourteenth century amounted to £15,000 (possibly £250 million in today's money). The priory is shown as it appeared at the time of its dissolution in November 1539, with the second illustration, a drawing dating to the early twentieth century, showing the remains of the Norman arches forming one of the walls of the chapter house. The entrance to the chapter house has been described as one of the mightiest pieces of early Norman architecture in England. (© Historic England Archive; Historic England Archive)

A Fragment of the Chapter House.

Below and opposite: Winchester Cathedral
A 1951 aerial view of the cathedral and the grounds (below) once occupied by the priory, with the claustral remains seen towards the centre of this photograph and around which other essential buildings, including the chapter house, library and dormitory, would have been situated. Opposite is a mid-twentieth-century view of the cathedral nave as seen from the choir. Originally built between 1079 and 1095, the cathedral was completely remodelled at the west end under Bishop Edington, with William of Wykeham continuing this work during the 1390s. (© Historic England Archive. Aerofilms Collection; Historic England Archive)

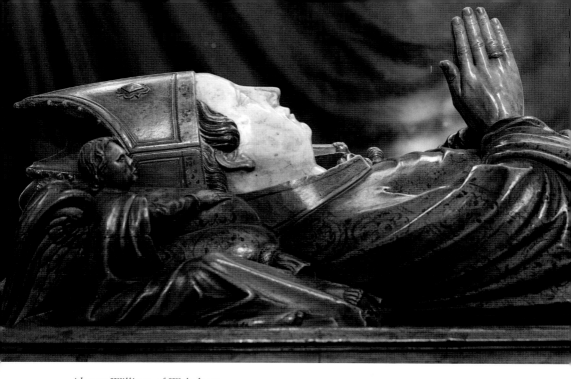

Above: William of Wykeham
The image above shows the tomb of William of Wykeham in the Wykeham Chantry Chapel of Winchester Cathedral. To help finance the remodelling of the cathedral as carried out by Wykeham, Bishop Edington left part of his wealth in his will for this purpose; however, most of the money needed came from the monastic estate and offerings made by pilgrims to saintly relics within the cathedral. (Historic England Archive)

Opposite below and right:
Augustinian Canonry at Portchester
The magnificent Norman church that stands within the outer bailey of Portchester Castle (opposite below) is all that remains of an Augustinian priory that was founded here by Henry I in around 1128. The cloisters of the priory were situated to the south, but no remains are discernible, although the position of the reredorter, or communal toilets, is visible in the fort wall. In the second photograph (right), taken in 1858, closer detail is shown of the Norman west doorway as built around 1133 for the Augustinian monks. (Author's collection; Historic England Archive)

Below: Southwick Priory
The Augustinians, whose priory had been founded by Henry I, remained at Portchester for only around twenty years, choosing to relocate themselves to a new priory that they had built at Southwick. The remaining above-ground evidence of that priory is restricted to part of the refectory wall, as seen here. (Author's collection)

Above: St Mary's Church, Basing

Although not part of a monastic establishment, the church at Basing once represented a different aspect of medieval cloistered society, the church being in the patronage of Mont Saint Michel Abbey in Lower Normandy. This meant that the abbey had the right to appoint priests to the church, a result of the Duke of Normandy, who had close associations with the abbey, also being the King of England during several reigns. The church itself probably began life as a timber structure, with the abbey responsible for its construction in stone sometime around 1089. Little remains from that very early period. (Historic England Archive)

Opposite below and above: Netley Abbey
Netley was a Cistercian abbey founded by Peter de Roches, Bishop of Winchester, in 1238.
The surviving ruins are quite substantial and permit a full appreciation of just how large
this monastic establishment was prior to its dissolution by Henry VIII. Despite the richness
of these buildings, the Order of Cistercians placed an emphasis on simplicity and poverty,
wearing habits of undyed wool. Following its dissolution, Netley Abbey was acquired by the
Marquess of Winchester, who converted the church and its ancillary buildings into a mansion
house. Continuing as such for around 150 years, the house was then abandoned and some of
the stonework removed, leaving the abbey in its present state and open to visitors. (© Historic
England Archive; Author's collection)

Above: South Transept and East Chancel, Netley Abbey
The ruins in this photograph are seen in a much earlier image, probably sometime during the 1860s, when an archaeological survey was underway (see photograph on page 12), conducted by Revds Edmund Kell and J. A. Addison. (Historic England Archive)

Above: Netley Abbey

An aerial view dating to 1951 and showing the extent of the abbey remains. During earlier times, many writers and artists of the romantic movement visited the site, which was then left open for anyone to visit, for the purpose of gaining inspiration and ideas. The foliage-covered buildings at that time did much to foster inspiration. (© Historic England Archive. Aerofilms Collection)

Opposite below: Chapter House, Netley Abbey

The arches of the chapter house. It was in the chapter house that daily meetings were held, with the abbey community gathering for religious readings prior to discussing the daily affairs of the abbey. The arches were designed to allow those outside the room to hear the discussions being held within. (Historic England Archive)

Left: Abbot's Lodging, Netley Abbey
The vaulted three-bay ground floor of an isolated building within the grounds of Netley Abbey are generally supposed to be the abbot's lodgings. In common with the other buildings of the abbey, the earlier foliage that gave a certain romantic image has been removed for the purpose of helping protect the various structures. (Author's collection)

Above and opposite below: Romsey Abbey

The abbey church at Romsey, the exterior view (on the previous page) of which dates to 1908. Early medieval in origin, it was first established as a nunnery in 907 by King Edward the Elder, son of Alfred the Great. At that time the church belonging to the foundation would have been a simple timber affair, with work on the present-day building beginning during the early part of the twelfth century. Through being one of the few established houses of the early Middle Ages, the nunnery, which adhered to the Rule of St Benedict, was presided over by the nobility, allowing them to send their daughters and those widowed to be educated. The future wife of Henry I, Matilda of Scotland, was educated at Romsey and a few years later a daughter of King Stephen was the abbess of the house. (Historic England Archive; Author's image)

Abbess's Doorway

This door, giving access into Romsey Abbey clearly dates from the Norman period and was positioned to allow the abbess of the monastery to enter the church directly from her lodgings. (Historic England Archive)

Right and opposite: Titchfield Abbey
Titchfield Abbey dates to the thirteenth
century when it was founded by canons of
the Premonstratensian Order, who served as
priests in local communities. This aerial view
(opposite) of 1951 shows the positioning
of some of the former Premonstratensian
abbey buildings by impressions on the
ground. Within the area of the cloister
and other parts of the former abbey,
medieval tiles, such as the one in the second
illustration (right), are still to be seen.
(© Historic England Archive. Aerofilms
Collection; © Historic England Archive)

Old Bishop's Palace, Winchester
Winchester was the richest medieval bishopric in the entire country – during the late fourteenth
century its various estates provided an income of approximately £40,000 per year (possibly
£680 million today). Much of this income was spent on supporting the bishop and his household,
with the Old Bishop's Palace in Winchester (Wolvesey Castle), of which only the ruins survive,
being just one of several residences possessed by the bishop. (© Historic England Archive)

The Palace in the Middle Ages
This illustration depicts the Old Bishop's Palace as it might have appeared during the twelfth century. Drawn by Philip Corke in 2008, it shows Bishop Henry de Blois (1129–71) presiding over a meeting of Church leaders in the East. It was Bishop de Blois who oversaw the building of much of the palace, including the east hall, a keep, a defensive tower and two gatehouses. (© Historic England Archive)

Above and below: Bishop's Waltham Palace
The Bishop of Winchester had the further residences of Farnham, Highclere and Bishop's Waltham – the latter two also in Hampshire. These two illustrations show the remains of the Great Hall of the palace at Bishop's Waltham, which was completed by Bishop William of Wykeham in 1381, replacing an earlier structure. The second shows the brewhouse and bakehouse, which, through being isolated from the Grand Hall, reduced the risk of any fire in this building spreading. The brew and bakehouse were a further addition to the palace made during the time of Wykeham. (Author's collection)

Castles, Forts and Defensive Walls

Portchester Castle and Roman Fort

Efforts to defend the coastal areas of Hampshire against foreign invasion have a long and fascinating history. Portchester Castle, seen here in this 1947 aerial photograph, has undertaken this role for around 1,500 years. Originally a Roman fortress, it was adapted by the Saxons and Normans, with further extensive alterations carried out in the fourteenth century. Even during the French wars of the eighteenth century it fulfilled an important role as a prison for captured enemy seamen. (© Historic England Archive. Aerofilms Collection)

Odiham Castle, North Warnborough
Constructed during the first two decades of the thirteenth century as a royal residence by King John, Odiham Castle has been in a state of ruin since at least 1603. The unusual octagonal keep lies on a tranquil site adjacent to the Basingstoke Canal, a contrast to the two-week siege that it witnessed in 1216 at the time of the First Barons' War. (© Historic England Archive. Aerofilms Collection)

Above and below: Winchester Castle
This was originally the site of defensive earthworks constructed by William the Conqueror immediately following his successful invasion, with a more substantial structure of stone added during the twelfth century. Seen here in 1926 is the Great Hall built by Henry III, one of the finest medieval aisled halls in the country and open to visitors most days, while the exterior view is a modern-day picture with the building ready for visitors. In the Long Gallery, accessed through the Great Hall, there is a display of material explaining the full history of the castle. (Historic England Archive; Author's image)

Above: Barracks, Winchester

Built on the site once occupied by the former area of the castle, the barracks at Winchester have variously been known as the Upper Barracks, the Peninsula Barracks and the Green Jackets Barracks. In 1994 the site was sold for residential development, although part of it was retained for a complex of military museums that includes, among others, the Royal Green Jacket (Rifles) Museum, the Royal Hampshire Regiment Museum and the Gurkha Museum. (Author's collection)

Above and previous page below: Southampton City Walls
Two turn-of-the-twentieth-century photographs of Southampton's medieval town walls. The masonry walls emerged out of defensive ditches and banks that first surrounded the growing town during the twelfth century. While no longer complete, the remaining sections of the walls are most impressive. In the second photograph, which dates to July 1906, an archway in the old town wall of Southampton, Blue Anchor Lane, is depicted. During the Second World War the city was subject to considerable bombing, with the walls once again serving to defend the civilian population from attack, this time as emergency air-raid shelters. (Historic England Archive)

Right and below: Hurst Castle
The aerial view of Hurst Castle dates to 1953, while the ground view is of the west wing as seen in 2012. Although considerably transformed between 1861 and 1874 by two extensive wings, the original structure dates to the reign of Henry VIII in response to a potential French invasion. It was one of a number of coast defence castles built by Henry, which are characterised by low bastions that would mount cannon more effectively and survive better when under attack by cannon fire. The west wing of Hurst Castle, as seen below, was added during the mid-nineteenth century and designed to mount shell-firing guns within granite casemates. Later, during the early twentieth century, the west wing was given the addition of quick-firing gun positions on the roof and a tower for the control and direction of gunnery. (© Historic England Archive. Aerofilms Collection; © Historic England Archive)

Left and below: Narrow-gauge Track, Hurst Castle
A narrow-gauge rail track was laid down within the castle for the purpose of hauling shells into the magazines that were located within the two wings. With an 18-inch gauge, the track ran from an unloading wharf through the length of the castle, briefly exiting at the centre point of the fortress to avoid the original Tudor castle before re-entering. While one picture shows detail of the track, the other shows the central magazine block with the rail line in the foreground. (© Historic England Archive)

Above and below: Calshot Castle

Viewed in 1888, Calshot Castle (above), as with Hurst, was also part of the coastal fortifications built by Henry VIII at the time of a threatened French invasion. Two other forts, also designed to protect the Solent, were built on the Isle of Wight at West and East Cowes. At the time of this photograph being taken, Calshot had long ceased having a military function and had been placed in the hands of the coastguard as a base to counter smuggling. The labelled map of the Solent is based on an Admiralty chart corrected to April 1893, with an inset map of Calshot Castle. By that date the castle had been returned to the War Office, with this map showing a series of projected works, including a gun battery yet to be built and to be armed with two 4.7-inch and four 12-pounder quick-firing guns, with searchlights to be positioned on the walls of the castle. (Historic England Archive)

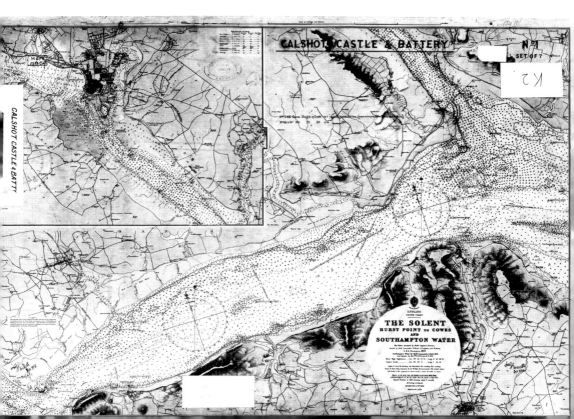

Above: Calshot Castle
An aerial view of Calshot Castle seen from the north-east and dating to 1928. By this date the castle had taken on a completely different role, serving the Royal Air Force as an experimental seaplane and testing station. Through its connections with seaplanes, Calshot was to achieve enduring fame by hosting the 1931 Schneider Trophy Race, which was won outright by Great Britain with the Supermarine S.6B. (© Historic England Archive. Aerofilms Collection)

Opposite above and below: Fort Cumberland, Portsmouth
A sketch map dating to 1820 showing the disposition of artillery in Fort Cumberland, which stands on the south-eastern corner of Portsmouth, at a time when the fort was armed with smoothbore cannon positioned to help prevent enemy ships passing through the channel leading into Langstone Harbour. The fort originally dates to the late 1740s, with construction overseen by the Duke of Cumberland, but was reconstructed in 1786. The second illustration shows a detail of one of the casemates, or fortified gun emplacement, of Fort Cumberland. Protected in 1964 as a scheduled monument, the fort is also Grade II* listed and is in the care of Historic England, serving as an archaeological research establishment. (Historic England Archive)

Sketch of Fort Cumberland, shewing
the Ordnance Land.

31st August 1820.

Scale of 10 feet to an Inch

4

5

UMBERLAND
MOUTH
HIRE

LEFT BASTION CASEMATES
EXTERNAL ELEVATION

SHEET NO. 4

LEFT BASTION

ENGLISH HERITAGE

PORTSMOUTH·SPITHEAD·DEFENCES

—OUTLINE · PLAN · SHEWING · SITE · OF—

FORT · CUMBERLAND

ISLE · OF · WIGHT

SPITHEAD

No.1.

No.16

A.

Above: Solent Sea Fort

The somewhat menacing appearance of one of the island-like sea forts in the Solent. Built during the second half of the nineteenth century, four sea forts were placed between the mainland of Hampshire and the Isle of Wight to protect the eastern approaches to Portsmouth Harbour. They were part of a ring of defences that surrounded Portsmouth and were the result of recommendations made by the Royal Commission on the defence of the United Kingdom, which first met in 1859. (Author's collection)

Opposite above: Hilsea Lines

Originally constructed during the eighteenth century, Hilsea Lines were designed to seal off Portsea Island from a land attack, but by the nineteenth century these were inadequate, with a more substantial ring of fortifications including the Gosport Advanced Line and forts along the line of Portsdown Hill providing a defence suited to the nature of weaponry then in use. Nevertheless, the Hilsea Lines were substantially strengthened during the mid-nineteenth century. This 1932 aerial view shows part of the Hilsea Lines, the east bastion, in the foreground while beyond is the one-time Portsmouth aerodrome. (© Historic England Archive. Aerofilms Collection)

Opposite below: Solent and Spithead Defences, 1886

This outline plan shows the defences around the important naval anchorage of Spithead, a stretch of water that also gave entrance into Portsmouth Harbour. Once a highly secret document, it was produced by the Board of Ordnance in 1886. Facing the Isle of Wight is Fort Cumberland and a series of batteries along the Portsea Island shoreline. Gosport is heavily fortified, as is the shoreline of the Isle of Wight, and within the waters of the Solent are a series of island forts. (© Historic England Archive)

Opposite above: Gosport Advanced Line
The need for such an extensive construction programme of fortifications during the mid-nineteenth century, designed to protect the dockyard and naval base at Portsmouth, had been prompted by a perceived, but unlikely, French invasion. To prevent Gosport falling into the hands of an enemy and thereby threatening Portsmouth from this direction, the Gosport Advanced Line, consisting of five large low-profile forts on the west side of Gosport, was built, of which this is an exterior view from the south of Fort Brockhurst. (© Historic England Archive)

Opposite below: Fort Brockhurst, Gosport
Orientation illustration depicting an aerial view of Fort Brockhurst as it appears in the present day, looking west with the fort's moated circular keep in the foreground. (© Historic England Archive)

Above: Fort Grange, Gosport
Fort Grange was part of the Gosport Advanced Line. Almost identical to Fort Brockhurst in design, an open area adjoining the fort was turned into an airfield just before the First World War, with the fort, as a result of this connection with aviation, being acquired by the RAF, who retained it until 1945 when it was transferred to the navy as HMS Siskin. Still in the hands of the Royal Navy, it now serves as a primary engineering training establishment under the name of HMS Sultan. (© Crown copyright. Historic England Archive)

Above: Portsdown Hill Forts

Along the line of Portsdown Hill, overlooking Portsmouth, five forts were constructed. These provided a further element in the ring of defences built to defend the naval base during the mid- to late nineteenth century. Following restoration Fort Nelson, seen here in this photograph of 2011, now houses part of the Royal Armouries collection within its 19 acres. (© Historic England Archive)

Below and opposite: Fort Purbrook

The five forts strung along the 6-mile ridge of Portsdown Hill are, from east to west, forts Purbrook, Widley, Southwick, Nelson and Wallington, with Fareham to the west acting as a connecting point between these five forts and those of the Gosport Advanced Line. These two illustrations of Fort Purbrook show the central courtyard of the barracks and a general view looking up through the spiral staircase to the barracks block. Positioned at the east end of the defensive line, Purbrook had a greater element of firepower that could be directed in a north-easterly direction, with further protection to the fort provided by two redoubts, Crookhorn and Farlington. (© Historic England Archive)

Town Houses

Above and opposite above: Medieval Merchant's House, Southampton
Built sometime around 1290, this was originally the house of a prosperous wine merchant, one of several similar houses that would have occupied the area of Southampton as a result of a thriving trade with other English possessions of that period and France. Now a popular visitor attraction, the house, as seen in this 1941 photograph, suffered during the German wartime bombing raids on the town. The age of the house and the realisation of its historical importance resulted in a determined effort to fully restore it after the war. Much of the early restoration work was carried out by the Department of the Environment before the house passed into the care of English Heritage, with the detailed study of the roof beams dating to the time when restoration work was underway in 1981. (Historic England Archive; © Crown copyright. Historic England Archive)

Opposite below: Cut-away Reconstruction of the Merchant's House
The Merchant's House is an important building, thought to be the earliest complete medieval house surviving in England. The drawing shows the underground storage cellar, over which the great hall is positioned, along with a shopfront looking out onto French Street. On the first floor are the bedchambers, with the one at the front projecting over the street, a commonly used method of gaining additional space in a densely populated area of town. (© Historic England Archive)

Left: God Begot House, High Street, Winchester
A four-storey, timber-framed, sixteenth-century residence with two front gables looking out onto the High Street. While the front of the building has been heavily restored, the side is much as it appeared when first built. This photograph dates from the mid-twentieth century, and the building is now a restaurant. (Historic England Archive)

Below: Nos 13–14 Cripstead Lane, St Cross, Winchester
Seen here under renovation in 1971, Nos 13–14 Cripstead Lane provides a splendid example of a now restored fifteenth- or sixteenth-century half-timbered two-storey cottage. Cripstead Lane itself is a road of considerable antiquity, once leading off from the king's highway to Crepestre Mill, on the side west of the River Itchen. The lane was certainly in existence during the early thirteenth century, with the possibility of it being of late Saxon origin. Nearby are an interesting collection of medieval and later houses. (© Crown copyright. Historic England Archive)

Above: Sheep Street, Petersfield
A group of timber-framed
sixteenth-century town houses in
Petersfield's Sheep Street, a road
so-named because it once held a
regular wool market and some of
the houses have connections with
the processing of wool. Carding, the
combing of wool into fibres ready
for spinning, is the name given to
one of the houses in Sheep Street.
(© Historic England Archive)

Right: Hyde House, Winchester
Seen here during the 1920s, Hyde
House is of the late seventeenth
century – note the Penfold
Victorian-era letter box on the right,
which has now been replaced by a
standard mid-twentieth-century-style
box. Of red brick, it has a distinctive
Dutch gable on the west elevation
facing onto Hyde Street and an ornate
brick doorway which is blocked up
(as seen in this illustration). (Historic
England Archive)

Left: Cheyney Court, Dome Alley,
The Close, Winchester
Adjoining the south entrance,
St Swithun's Gate, and leading
into the Cathedral Close, this is a
1947 view of the corner of Cheyney
Court seen from the north-east.
Once the Bishop's Court House, the
house dates to the fifteenth century
but was considerably enlarged
during the late seventeenth century.
(Historic England Archive)

Above: Serle's House, Southgate Street, Winchester

Now housing the museum of the Royal Hampshire Regiment, Serle's House dates to the first half of the eighteenth century. Set back from the road, it is a red-brick building with blue dressings and is of appreciable size – having seven bays and three storeys with the three central bays projecting outwards. Named after the Serle family, the house was purchased by attorney James Serle in 1781, with the house later occupied by his son Peter who, in turn, sold the property to the government in 1796. (Author's collection)

Opposite below: Lombard Street, Portsmouth

Seen here are a group of two-storey town houses of the late seventeenth century with Dutch gable roofs. Immediately adjoining are two houses of the late Georgian period with first-floor bay windows. The fact of their continued survival into the present century is owed to a degree of fortuity, with this photograph from October 1943 demonstrating the extensive damage that wartime bombing inflicted upon this area of Portsmouth. The flattened buildings facing this range have now been replaced by Lombard Court – a somewhat more modern design. (Historic England Archive)

Madeline House, Bishops Waltham
One of several former Georgian residences, Madeline House is seen here in 1942. By then it had its ground floor converted into two shops. A similar picture today would show the further conversion of the building into one ground-floor shop, but the remainder of the exterior has hardly changed. (Historic England Archive)

Right: Lansdowne House, High Street, Alton
Now a bank, Lansdowne House is a
particularly attractive mid-eighteenth-century
former residence, with this photograph
taken on 5 May 1921. A particular feature
of the building is its deep, moulded and
dentilled eaves cornice, a feature based
on Italian Renaissance architecture.
(Historic England Archive)

Below: Eastbrook House,
The Square, Wickham
Little has changed since this photograph
was taken in 1921. Eastbrook House was
originally built in the seventeenth century,
but the frontage, as seen here, is primarily of
the eighteenth century. The oriel window on
the first floor and resting on a colonnaded
open porch adds particular distinction.
(Historic England Archive)

Grand Houses

Right and opposite: The Vyne, Sherborne
St John, near Basingstoke

Two exterior views of the north façade of
The Vyne, a former Tudor mansion built
for Sir William Sandys between 1500 and
1520, replacing a much smaller house. His
son, William, the 1st Baron Sandys, Lord
Chancellor and favourite of Henry VIII,
greatly improved the mansion, with further
substantial additions being carried out during
the seventeenth, eighteenth and nineteenth
centuries. The house is now in the ownership of
the National Trust. While the first illustration
is a general view of The Vyne, the second is a
more detailed study of the portico designed by
the English architect John Webb and dating
to the year 1654. Adhering to the Corinthian
style, it is a piece of work of considerable
importance – it is the first example of a
classical-style portico on an English country
house. (Historic England Archive)

Grand Hall of The Vyne

Another significant addition to The Vyne
was carried out by notable architect John
Chute, whose family owned The Vyne
during the eighteenth century. This was the
spectacular staircase within the former great
hall, seen from the central landing with its
coffered ceiling. In appearance, a design
described by the English statesman Robert
Walpole as being in the manner of a theatrical
stage, it has no rival in any other English
country house. (Historic England Archive)

Above: Titchfield Abbey
Following the Dissolution of the Monasteries part of the abbey at Titchfield was converted into a mansion, with the gatehouse (seen here) built across the nave of the abbey church. (Historic England Archive)

Opposite: Warblington Castle
Little remains of this large moated house built by Margaret Pole, Countess of Salisbury, towards the beginning of the sixteenth century. Ruined during the Civil War, all that remains is one of the octagonal brick turrets of the gatehouse and part of a wall. It is close to the parish church but within the area of a privately owned farm. (Author's image)

Above: Beaulieu Abbey
A photograph taken in 1890 of Beaulieu Abbey house from across the lake. The abbey, after which it takes its name, was founded by King John in 1204 for Cistercian monks, with the house once forming the gatehouse. Purchased, following the Dissolution of the Monasteries, by Sir Thomas Wriothesley, the future 1st Earl of Southampton, it passed through marriage to the Montagu family, who are still in possession of the house and its estate. During the Second World War, Beaulieu and its grounds served as a training establishment for the Special Operations Executive (SOE). (Historic England Archive)

Opposite above and below: Highclere Castle
Originally built as a plain, eighteenth-century mansion, the exterior of Highclere was refaced by Sir Charles Barry in 1839–42. Barry was working on the design and construction of the Houses of Parliament at the same time as working on Highclere and the house, with its corner turrets and central tower, shows distinct similarities. The aerial view was taken in August 1928. (Historic England Archive; © Historic England Archive. Aerofilms Collection)

Winchester Barracks 1850

Below: Stargrove, East Woodhay

A mid-nineteenth-century baronial-style chateau seen here *c.* 1914. Once the home of rock star Mick Jagger, for a time the house served as a recording studio for various bands. During the 1970s the estate was used to film two serials of the BBC television series *Doctor Who*. (Historic England Archive)

Above: Hinton Ampner House, Bramdean
Only a cellar remains of the original residence built here sometime around 1800, with a house designed in the neo-Georgian style replacing it in 1937. In turn, though, this suffered greatly in a fire that broke out in 1960, leading to its remodelling at that time, with an Adam ceiling fortunately surviving. (© Historic England Archive)

Opposite above: King's House, Winchester
On part of the site of Winchester Castle following its destruction on the orders of Oliver Cromwell, construction began of a Christopher Wren-designed grand house for Charles II, a summer residence for the court known as the King's House. Unfinished at the time of Charles II's death, and never serving its original purpose, the King's House saw various alternative uses, including housing both French prisoners of war and French priests escaping the revolution in France and as a military barracks. Demolished following a fire in December 1894, a new military building – the Upper Barracks, later Peninsula Barracks – was constructed on the site once occupied by the King's House and built in a similar style. (Historic England Archive)

Above: Broadlands House
The home of Earl and Countess Mountbatten of Burma and the birthplace of nineteenth-century prime minister Viscount Palmerston, Broadlands was built in the sixteenth century but refaced from around 1767, giving it a Palladian-style appearance. Clearly seen in this 1925 aerial photograph are the grounds as laid out by 'Capability' Brown and the east front of the house with its central three-bay portico with pediment. (© Historic England Archive. Aerofilms Collection)

Opposite above: The Grange, The Grange Park, Northington
During the first decade of the eighteenth century, this fairly modest brick house was transformed, giving it the appearance of an ancient Greek temple. Strangely heavy in appearance, the Parthenon-style portico was formed of eight Greek Doric columns. It is one of the finest examples of Greek Revival architecture in Europe and an important example of the trend, common in the aristocracy, to celebrate all things reflecting classical Greece in this period. (Historic England Archive)

Opposite below: Southwick House, Southwick
While formerly a grand residence built around 1800, Southwick has been a military establishment since 1940, formerly requisitioned in 1941. In the months leading up to D-Day much of the planning for the invasion of Europe was undertaken here, having become the headquarters of the main Allied commanders, with General Eisenhower and General Montgomery frequently here. Nowadays, it is the home of the Defence School of Policing and Guarding but is to be sold by the Ministry of Defence in 2025. (© Crown copyright Historic England Archive)

Local Villages

South Warnborough

In this view of South Warnborough it is possible to gain a feel of how village life might once have been in rural Hampshire. It is a view looking towards Lees Hill and the Old Police Cottage – yes, most villages once had a local 'bobby'. The photograph is one of a series taken for the auctioneers Daniel Smith, Oakley and Garrard in May 1921 when the 1,120-acre South Warnborough estate was about to be auctioned. The sale included the manor house, a chalk pit, New Farm and Ford Farm. (Historic England Archive)

Swan Green
One of the most picturesque locations in the New Forest, Swan Green, with its thatched cottages, lies within a short distance of Lyndhurst. Here, Beehive Cottage, a two-storey thatched lodge, photographed in the 1960s, is seen. Beehive Cottage was built in the late eighteenth century and extended in the nineteenth century, and is now Grade II listed. (© Historic England Archive)

Above and previous page below: Corhampton

Proof that either a small hamlet or village has existed at Corhampton for at least a thousand years, this church is clearly of Saxon origin, and was possibly built during the first quarter of the eleventh century. Not to be missed, carved into the wall to the right of the porch is a Saxon sundial. The yew tree overshadowing the church is also of ancient date, estimated to be at least 1,200 years old. Internally, the church has a Saxon chancel arch, which follows the Saxon style of being formed from plain blocks and undecorated slabs at the head of the two columns. (Author's collection)

Opposite above and below: Hursley

Hursley, which lies between Winchester and Romsey, is seen here in two turn-of-the-twentieth-century views. At that time, villages were often self-sustaining communities providing work for both the skilled and unskilled as well as the occasional professional. A delivery van is seen passing along the main street heading towards the smithery, which lies immediately behind the photographer, with both the smith and the carter examples of that vibrant village economy – the carter was essential for bringing everyday items into the village and the smith to repair farm machinery. In the second view of Hursley, the large house belongs to the doctor. At one time it would have been common for villages to have had a doctor whose house would have served as a small surgery, but prior to the creation of the NHS, each visit would result in a payment being made, which varied from one doctor to another. Those with a village practice were likely to know each of their patients by name. (Historic England Archive)

Above: Minstead

Few villages, either now or in the past, would be without a drinking tavern or public house. Seen here in the village of Minstead, which lies to the north of Lyndhurst in the New Forest, is The Trusty Servant. Photographed in 1908, the building, which faces the village green and still serves hungry and thirsty customers, dates back to the eighteenth century. The author Arthur Conan Doyle is buried in the churchyard at Minstead, his gravestone reading 'Steel true/Blade straight/ Arthur Conan Doyle/Knight/Patriot, Physician, and man of letters'. (Historic England Archive)

Opposite above: Chesapeake Mill, Wickham

Dating to around 1820, the watermill at Wickham is so named due to being constructed from the timbers of the United States' thirty-eight-gun frigate *Chesapeake*, which was captured in battle by HMS *Shannon* during the war of 1812. This was not unusual in the sense that naval warships of this period, when seen as having no further use by the Admiralty, were dismantled and the timber from which they had been built were sold to the highest bidder – in the case of *Chesapeake*, her timbers were purchased for £500. No longer operating as a mill, the building houses an eclectic collection of lifestyle antiques and collectibles. (© Crown copyright. Historic England Archive)

Above and previous page below: Langstone
Several Hampshire villages emerged during later periods to meet the needs of particular trades. One such example is Langstone, lying at the eastern extreme of the county alongside Chichester Harbour, which developed in the early nineteenth century as a small port to meet the immediate needs of other communities in the area. Imports, for instance, included coal for household consumption and manure for use on farms. A particular feature of the village was the mill, seen here in June 1939, by which time it had ceased functioning. Through being situated close by the water, barges could be brought up to the mill for loading, taking the grain that had been milled to various destinations. (Author's collection; Historic England Archive)

Opposite above and below: Buckler's Hard
Two contrasting views of Buckler's Hard. The first is a photograph taken in 1906 of the terraced cottages of the village with the River Beaulieu in the distance; the more recent view shows Buckler's Hard from the south in 2010. While originally planned as a major port town, which failed to develop, an alternative shipbuilding enterprise brought considerable work to the area during the eighteenth and early nineteenth centuries, with ships built here including three large warships that served Nelson in 1805 at the Battle of Trafalgar: *Agamemnon*, *Euryalus* and *Swiftsure*. (Historic England Archive; © Historic England Archive)

Above: Netley
A further Hampshire village that emerged to meet a particular situation is Netley, seen here in 1909. The terraced houses date to the late nineteenth century when a village community began to develop in response to the needs of the nearby military hospital, with a further boost to growth created by the arrival of a railway and the building of a station during the 1860s. (Historic England Archive)

Left: Upper Farringdon
An unusual feature to be found in Farringdon, a village south of Alton, is Massey's Folly, a substantial red-brick building that was built by Thomas Hackett Massey, aided by occasional skilled artisans and labourers. Eclipsing the original village, it seems to have had no specific purpose other than to keep Massey, the village rector from 1857 to 1919, occupied. It did find later use as the village school. (© Historic England Archive)

Health During Wartime

Above and below: Royal Naval Hospital, Haslar, Gosport

Under 'Archaeology', the more than 20,000 seamen and marines buried in the cemetery of this hospital have already been referred to, providing evidence, albeit somewhat sad, of the role Haslar once played in supporting the sick and wounded of the Royal Navy. No longer a hospital, a number of the impressive buildings still remain. The upper photograph shows one such building in a view looking along an arched passage in the north entrance of the former hospital. The lower photograph is a view of the north-east side of the hospital, which was completed by 1753 during the reign of George II. In recognition of this, the decorative tympanum has George II's coat of arms as well as allegorical figures and emblems depicting Navigation and Commerce, emphasising naval links and the expansion of the British Empire through overseas trade. Much of the rest of the hospital was not complete until 1761. (© Historic England Archive)

Above and left: Royal Victoria Hospital, Netley
The construction of the Royal Victoria Hospital at Netley was prompted by the appalling conditions of medical treatment provided for those soldiers injured in the Crimean War of 1854 to 1856. Construction of the hospital was started in 1856 and it went on to play an important part in treating the wounded of both the First and Second World Wars. No longer in existence, and now demolished, an idea of the extent of the former hospital, which was once a quarter of a mile long, can be gauged from this aerial view from 1923. Following the demolition of the hospital, the site has been transformed into the Royal Victoria Country Park, with only the former hospital chapel, as seen in the second picture, still remaining. (© Historic England Archive. Aerofilms Collection; Author's image)

Royal South Hampshire and Southampton Hospital

The war that broke out in September 1939 would place considerable strain on the Royal South Hampshire and Southampton Hospital, as it was then known. Southampton was heavily bombed, suffering over fifty air raids and some 2,300 high-explosive bombs. Here, in October 1938, just eleven months before the outbreak of war, nurses at the hospital examine a gift of Dresden china that was sent to the hospital by HM Queen Mary, which was to be sold at a bazaar in aid of the Hospital Centenary Appeal Fund. (Historic England Archive)

Royal Hampshire County Hospital, Winchester

The accommodation needed for a considerable increase of nurses that would be required during the wartime period was fortuitously assisted by the opening, in June 1939, of a new nurses' home at the Royal Hampshire County Hospital. Seen here prior to its opening by the Duchess of Kent, the home was built at a cost of £20,000. (Historic England Archive)

Above and left: Sir Harold Gillies, Pioneering Reconstructive Surgeon Sir Harold Gillies was a pioneering plastic surgeon and consultant advisor to the Ministry of Health, who undertook what was referred to as aesthetic reconstructive surgery upon patients with disfiguring injuries. During the Second World War much of his work was undertaken at Rooksdown House, north-west of Basingstoke. The private wing of Park Prewett Mental Hospital, Rooksdown House had been converted into a plastic surgery unit in 1940 to treat service and civilian casualties. In these two photographs, part of a set dating to March 1942, patients are seen in the grounds of the unit and at mealtime. (Historic England Archive)

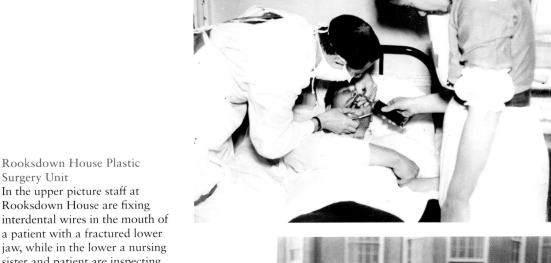

Rooksdown House Plastic Surgery Unit
In the upper picture staff at Rooksdown House are fixing interdental wires in the mouth of a patient with a fractured lower jaw, while in the lower a nursing sister and patient are inspecting a rose bush in the grounds of the unit. Outside of the hospital patients often experienced negative reactions to their disfigurement. The hospital attempted to counter this through the formation of the Rooksdown Club, which kept patients and staff in contact with one another, helped with welfare matters and attempted to educate the public about disfigurement. (Historic England Archive)

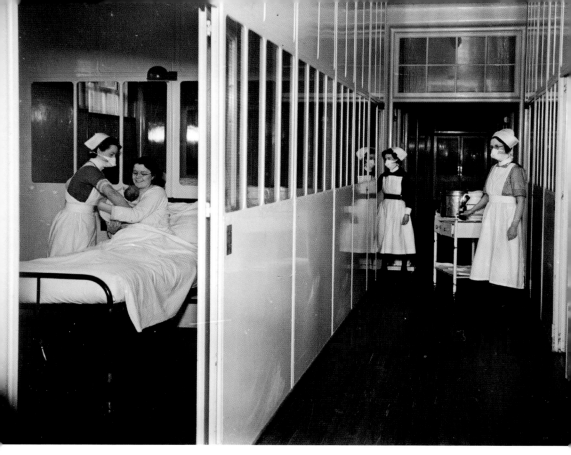

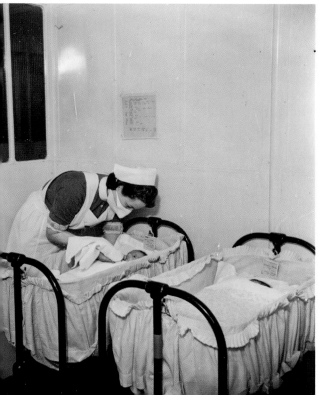

Above and left: St Mary's Hospital, Milton Road, Portsmouth
Even in wartime life sometimes went on as normal, with hospitals not only having to aid the sick and wounded but attending to the happier event of bringing new babies into the world. These two photographs, both dating to March 1942, show the maternity block at St Mary's Hospital, a large newly converted ward in the hospital. Also during the 1940s, a maternity home in the Hampshire countryside had been opened as an annexe. (Historic England Archive)

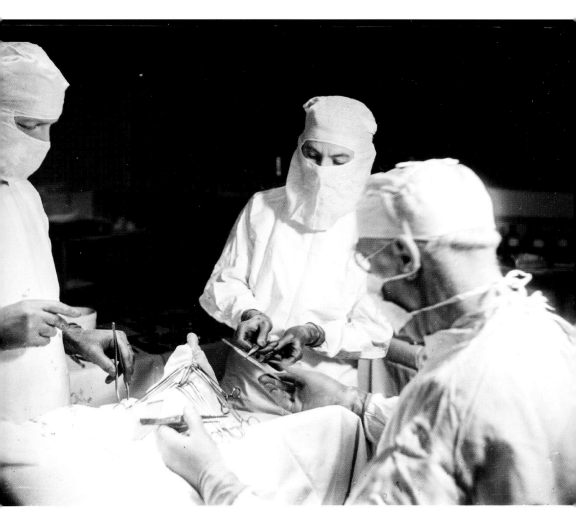

Lord Mayor Treloar Hospital, Alton
A hospital established in 1907 for the treatment and support of disabled children, a sister at the Treloar Hospital is photographed in December 1942 passing an instrument with forceps to the surgeon as a demonstration of the 'non-touch technique' practice of surgery. This was a method in which a gloved finger was never allowed to come into contact with the wound or with anything introduced into it because gloves were not reliable and perforations were possible. All instruments were long so as to keep surgeons' hands away from the wound, and theatre nurses held and prepared instruments using forceps. (Historic England Archive)

Above and left: Mobile Infant Welfare Unit

As a consequence of the intensive bombing raids mounted on both Portsmouth and Southampton during the Second World War, a mobile infant welfare unit (created in January 1942) was given to the county of Hampshire by Boots, a company that also maintained and staffed the unit. It could travel to areas where air raids and bombing had disrupted regular child welfare services. Short training courses were provided and successful candidates were awarded a certificate. The smaller runabout and stores van seen in the upper picture was known as *Nannie III*. (Historic England Archive)

Work and Leisure

Farming
Traditionally, many rural areas in Hampshire were reliant on agriculture, but the twentieth century witnessed a decline in its importance, with only 1.32 per cent of the county's rural population now dependent on farming as a source of employment. In May 1956, *Country Fair* magazine featured this picture of Mr E. F. Munday driving his tractor on a farm in Binstead, east of Alton. (© Historic England Archive)

Hopping
It was during the nineteenth century that hop growing peaked in Hampshire, with 3,200 acres at one time devoted to it. Here, during the 1960s, a farmer is seen setting the strings to the hop poles on an east Hampshire hop field. (© Historic England Archive)

Above: Carting
While goods vehicles are predominantly employed in the twenty-first century for the transporting of farm produce, in earlier times, such as in this 1906 view overlooking the River Beaulieu near Buckler's Hard, agriculture produce was moved by horse and cart, riverboats and barges. (Historic England Archive)

Below and opposite above: Dairy Farming
The dairy of Minley Home Farm, part of Minley Manor, was part of a purpose-built farm with an ideal layout, consequently becoming known as a 'Model Farm'. Designed by architect Arthur Castings, these two photographs, both taken in October 1906 shortly after the dairy's completion, show products on display and give a view of the stables. (Historic England Archive)

Below: Industrial Southampton
While many rural villages in Hampshire once possessed, through farming and related trades, a virtual self-contained economy, large towns and cities such as Gosport, Portsmouth and Southampton, while also being one time dependent on agriculture, had moved in very different directions. Southampton, for its part, offered considerable employment through being developed as a major port town. This 1946 aerial view shows RMS *Queen Elizabeth* at the New or Western Docks, which opened in 1934. (© Historic England Archive. Aerofilms Collection)

Above and below: Two Naval Towns

For Gosport and Portsmouth it was the Admiralty that became the largest employer, with the connection highlighted by occasional fleet reviews held in the Spithead Waters, which could easily be seen from both towns. This aerial photo (above) is of the fleet review held off Gosport in 1924. Not surprisingly, within these two towns memorials to the navy and its personnel abound, including this wall-mounted centenary plaque at the Haslar Royal Naval Hospital commemorating the Royal Naval Sick Berth Branch, which was founded in 1884. The inscription reads: 'To commemorate the centenary of the Royal Naval Sick Berth Branch, established by order in council on 17 October 1884. This plaque was unveiled by the Earl of Winchelsea and Nottingham on Sunday 26 August 1984.' (© Historic England Archive. Aerofilms Collection; © Historic England Archive)

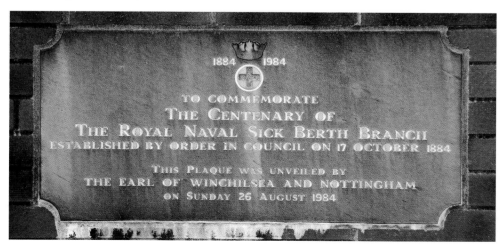

Above and right: Aeronautical Engineering at Farnborough

At the beginning of the twentieth century, Farnborough introduced an entirely new industry to the county in the form of aeronautics. Apart from the manufacture of aircraft, Farnborough developed an expertise in research and development. In the upper of these two photographs, this one dating to 1924, the building visible housed a seaplane tank used for testing float designs for aircraft alighting and taking-off from water. The second is a 1998 photograph of the Q121, the low-speed 24-foot wind tunnel built during the 1930s and used to test the likely performance and airflow over a new scaled-down design in simulated flight conditions. (© Crown copyright. Historic England Archive)

Urban Employment
As the larger towns in Hampshire continued to grow, they also created additional employment in the form of various services to support the increasing numbers drawn into these urban centres. Transport is one obvious example. This 1928 aerial view shows the Gosport Tramways Power Station in Fareham, built between 1903 and 1904. (© Historic England Archive. Aerofilms Collection)

The Workhouse
The union workhouses were among the most hated institutions in the county, designed, when first established during the 1830s, as a punishment for those who were without paid employment or other means of income. By making life uncomfortable, the government thought it would force the unemployed to find work to avoid the workhouse. It was false thinking, however: if the jobs were not there, it was not possible to find work. Seen here in 1991, this is part of a former workhouse building in Romsey – now Hayter House. (© Crown copyright. Historic England Archive)

Middle-class Relaxation
While town pubs sometimes acquired an unwholesome reputation, the village pub, especially in the more affluent areas of the county, presented, and still present, a very different image. There can be no mistaking the more affluent background of these folk seen in a Hampshire village pub, possibly Old Basing – it's the spaniel hogging the fireplace that is the real giveaway.
(© Historic England Archive)

Old World Tea Garden
A pleasant way of spending some leisure time would be a short stopover at a tearoom such as this one, the Old World Tea Garden in Boldre. Such venues became especially popular upon the arrival of the motor car and the subsequent ease of getting into the countryside.
(Historic England Archive)

COTTAGE AND OLD WORLD TEA GARDEN, PASSFORD FARM, LYMINGTON, HANTS.

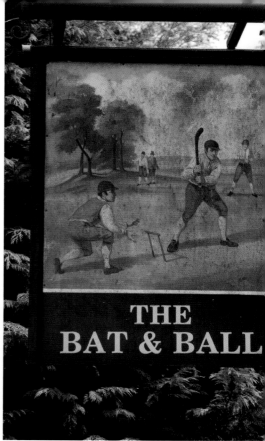

Above and opposite below: Cricket – Amateur and Professional

Whether on the local recreation ground of Broadhalfpenny Down, within the castle grounds of Portchester during the summer of 1930 (as seen in the lower picture on the previous page), or the County Ground, as seen in this aerial photograph in 1951, cricket has long proved a popular leisure activity in the county. In the year 2000, after 115 years, the County Ground saw its last county cricket match and the Hampshire County Cricket Club moved to a new ground, the Rose Bowl (currently the Ageas Bowl). (Historic England Archive; © Historic England Archive. Aerofilms Collection)

Opposite above left and right: The Hambledon Club

Though cricket had been around for many years, the Hambledon Club was a social club famous for its organisation of cricket matches and by 1770 it was the foremost cricket club in the country. The club's popularity grew due to its exclusive membership of noblemen and country gentry, driven by the added excitement of betting on winning teams. Commemorating Hambledon's connection with cricket are the local pub and a monument on the village's Broadhalfpenny Down Cricket Ground. (© Historic England Archive)

Above and below: Real Tennis
Still popular on Hayling Island was real tennis, the original indoor racket sport. It is played at the island's Seacourt clubhouse in Victoria Avenue. The clubhouse is seen here as it appeared in 1911, viewed across the croquet lawn; the photograph below, also dating to 1911, shows members of the club posing alongside the real tennis court. (Historic England Archive)

Above and right: The
Pier at Lee-on-the-Solent
In summer, of course,
the coastal resorts of
Hampshire come into
their own, but were
especially popular
during the first half of
the twentieth century.
At Lee-on-the-Solent,
not one of the most
well-known of resorts,
a Victorian pier existed
up until the Second
World War. This
aerial view (above) of
Lee-on-the-Solent pier
was taken in 1928,
while the view along the
pier (right) was taken in
1936. (Historic England
Archive)

The Beach
For those who wish to get their feet wet in summer, the Hampshire coastline has no shortage of beaches. This aerial view along the beach at Hayling Island dates to 1950. Here the magnificent sands that look out over the English Channel helped ensure that the one-time hamlet of West Town grew into a popular resort with a parade along the south beach. (© Historic England Archive. Aerofilms Collection)

The Farnborough Air Show
While Farnborough and its airfield might be a workplace for some, for others it offered, and continues to offer, the excitement of an air show that was once held annually (now bi-annually). Here, for the amusement of spectators, both those in the trade and those who were not, the cream of British aviation filled the air. Without a doubt, the Farnborough Air Show in the 1950s and 1960s was without parallel for Britain then was at the forefront of world aviation, with new aircraft constantly being showcased, as seen in this 1952 aerial view. (© Historic England Archive. Aerofilms Collection)

Above and below: Theatregoing

These images show two theatres highly popular in their day: the Castle Theatre, which occupied the second floor of the keep at Portchester Castle (above), and the Aldershot Hippodrome. The first is a reconstructed drawing of how the Castle Theatre's interior may have appeared when it was established at the beginning of the nineteenth century, possibly at a time when the castle was used as a Napoleonic War prison camp. The Hippodrome, looking down from the auditorium towards the stage, is seen at the time of its first opening in February 1913 when twice-nightly variety shows regularly had a packed house. (© Historic England Archive; Historic England Archive)

Above and opposite: The Picture House
The arrival of movies transformed the world of entertainment, with the towns of Hampshire often boasting several picture houses, while even larger villages often possessed a small cinema. Andover, a military town, was no exception, gaining its first picture palace in 1911. However, it is Andover's Odeon, which began life in 1926 as the Palace, that is seen in this photograph (opposite) taken in July 1937, shortly after its acquisition by Odeon. It is now a Mecca Bingo club. The above illustration is an interior view of Winchester's Picture House, the first purpose-built cinema to open in the city, opening on 14 April 1914. It is seen here shortly after its closure in March 1936, the building, which still survives, having been sold. (Historic England Archive)

About the Author

Philip MacDougall writes books for Amberley Publishing on southern England, and has a particular interest in the military and naval complexes that arose in and around Hampshire. As a social historian, he is interested in the people and the resources of those areas and the support they provided for those military complexes. That interest was possibly first sparked by having a distant ancestor who served as Nelson's secretary during the 1790s. As well as being an author, Philip has contributed biographical material on selected naval officers for the widely acclaimed Dictionary of National Biography. A speaker at events, both local and national, he offers a wide range of talks in connection with the books he has written.

About the Archive

Many of the images in this volume come from the Historic England Archive, which holds over 12 million photographs, drawings, plans and documents covering England's archaeology, architecture, social and local history.

The photographic collections include prints from the earliest days of photography to today's high-resolution digital images. Subjects range from Neolithic flint mines and medieval churches to art deco cinemas and 1980s shopping centres. The collection is a vivid record both of buildings that are still part of everyday life – places of work, leisure and worship – and those lost long ago, surviving only in fragile prints or glass-plate negatives.

Six million aerial photographs offer a unique and fascinating view of the transformation of England's towns, cities, coast and countryside from 1919 onwards. Highlights include the pioneering photography of Aerofilms, and the comprehensive survey of England captured by the RAF after the Second World War.

Plans, drawings and reports provide further context and reconstruction artworks bring archaeological sites and historic buildings to life.

The collections are housed in a purpose-built environmentally controlled store in Swindon, which provides the best conditions to preserve archive items for future generations to enjoy. You can search our catalogue online, see and buy copies of our images, as well as visiting our public search room by appointment.

Find out more about us at HistoricEngland.org.uk/Photos
email: archive@historicengland.org.uk
tel.: 01793 414600

The Historic England offices and archive store in Swindon from the air, 2007.